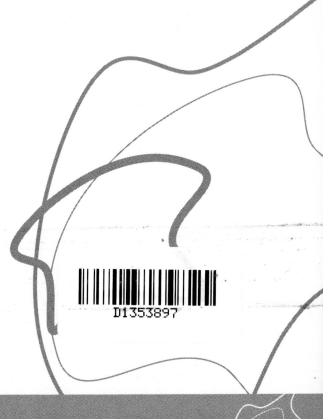

D1353897

Succeed at psychometric testing

PRACTICE TESTS FOR
DATA
INTERPRETATION

New edition

Succeed at psychometric testing

PRACTICE TESTS FOR
DATA
INTERPRETATION

HODDER
EDUCATION
PART OF HACHETTE LIVRE UK

New edition

Sally Vanson

The publisher has used its best endeavours to ensure that the URLs for external websites referred to in this book are correct and active at the time of going to press. However, the publisher and the author have no responsibility for the websites and can make no guarantee that the site will remain live or that the content will remain relevant, decent or appropriate.

Orders: please contact Bookpoint Ltd, 130 Milton Park, Abingdon, Oxon OX14 4SB. Telephone: (44) 01235 827720. Fax: (44) 01235 400454. Lines are open from 9.00–5.00, Monday to Saturday, with a 24-hour message answering service. You can also order through our website www.hoddereducation.co.uk.

British Library Cataloguing in Publication Data
A catalogue record for this title is available from the British Library.

ISBN: 978 0 340 96928 1

First Published 2004
Second edition 2008
Impression number   10 9 8 7 6 5 4 3
Year   2012 2011 2010 2009

Copyright © 2004, 2008 Sally Vanson

Typeset by Servis Filmsetting Ltd, Longsight, Manchester.
Printed in Great Britain for Hodder Education, part of Hachette Livre UK, 338 Euston Road, London NW1 3BH by Cox & Wyman Ltd, Reading, Berkshire.

Hachette Livre UK's policy is to use papers that are natural, renewable and recyclable products and made from wood grown in sustainable forests. The logging and manufacturing processes are expected to conform to the environmental regulations of the country of origin.

CONTENTS

Acknowledgements   vi

Foreword   vii

Chapter 1: Introduction   1

Chapter 2: Timed tests   21

Chapter 3: Answers to and explanations of timed tests   119

Chapter 4: Diagnosis and further reading   135

ACKNOWLEDGEMENTS

The following tests are reproduced with kind permission:

Test One, Questions 1 and 2, SHL; Test Four, Procter and Gamble

FOREWORD

Should anyone tell you that a psychometric test will give an accurate indication of your level of intelligence, don't pay too much attention. It isn't necessarily true.

The credibility of the global psychometric testing industry rests on the belief of employers that a psychometric test will yield accurate and reliable data about a candidate's ability. Busy employers buy into the notion that a psychometric test will swiftly eliminate all the unsuitable candidates and deliver up only the best, brightest and most able candidates to the interview stage.

What is not widely known is that it is perfectly possibly for a candidate to drastically improve their own psychometric score by adopting a methodical approach to test preparation. The purpose of the *Succeed at Psychometric Testing* series is to provide you with the necessary tools for this purpose.

It is useful to know that a candidate's ability to perform well in a psychometric test is determined by a wide range of factors, aside from the difficulty of the questions in the test. External factors include the test environment and the professionalism of the test administrator; internal factors relate to the candidate's confidence level on the day, the amount of previous test practice the candidate has and the candidate's self-belief that they will succeed. While you cannot always control the external factors, you can manage many of the internal factors.

A common complaint from test takers is the lack of practice material available to them. The titles in the *Succeed at Psychometric Testing* series address this gap and the series is designed with you, the test taker in mind. The content focuses on practice and explanations rather than on the theory and science. The authors are all experienced test takers and understand the benefits of thorough test preparation. They have prepared the content with the test taker's priorities in mind. Research has shown us that test takers don't have much notice of their test, so they need lots of practice, right now, in an environment that simulates the real test as closely as possible.

In all the research for this series, I have met only one person who likes – or rather, doesn't mind – taking psychometric tests. You are not alone. This person is a highly successful and senior manager in the NHS and she has taken psychometric tests for many of the promotions for which she has applied. Her attitude to the process is sanguine: 'I have to do it, I can't get out of it and I want the promotion so I might as well get on with it.' She always does well. A positive mental attitude is absolutely crucial in preparing yourself for your upcoming test and will undoubtedly help you on the day. If you spend time practising beforehand and become familiar with the format of the test, you are already in charge of some of the factors that deter other candidates on the day.

It's worth bearing in mind that the skills you develop in test preparation will be useful to you in your everyday life and in your new job. For many people, test preparation is not the most joyful way to spend free time, but know that by doing so, you are not wasting your time.

The *Succeed at Psychometric Testing* series covers the whole spectrum of skills and tests presented by the major test publishers and will help you prepare for your numerical, verbal, logical, abstract and diagrammatic reasoning tests. The series now also includes a title on personality testing. This new title will help you understand the role that personality testing plays in both the recruitment process and explains how such tests can also help you to identify areas of work to which you, personally, are most suited. The structure of each title is designed to help you to mark your practice tests quickly and find an expert's explanation to the questions you have found difficult.

If you don't attain your best score at your first attempt, don't give up. Book yourself in to retake the test in a couple of months, go away and practise the tests again. Psychometric scores are not absolute and with practice, you can improve your score.

Good luck! Let us know how you get on.

Heidi Smith, Series Editor
educationenquiries@hodder.co.uk

Other titles in the series:

Critical Verbal Reasoning
Diagrammatic and Abstract Reasoning
National Police Selection Process
Numerical Reasoning Intermediate
Numerical Reasoning Advanced
Personality Testing
Verbal Reasoning Intermediate
Verbal Reasoning Advanced

CHAPTER ONE
INTRODUCTION

Psychometric tests can be traced back to Hippocrates in 400 BC when he started trying to identify temperament types. From this early work, two types of test have developed, building on the work of Sir Francis Gatton in the 19th century who tried to show that the human mind was multi-dimensional. It is the work of Francis Gatton and his French colleague Binet which influenced the psychometrics we use today. The two types of test are concerned with personality definition and with measuring aptitude. The professional body in the United Kingdom with responsibility for managing best practice in the use of tests, the British Psychological Society (BPS), describes psychometric tests as 'an instrument designed to produce a quantitive assessment of some psychological attribute or attributes'.

Modern psychometric testing, which originated in the UK as part of recruitment assessment centres for the Royal Navy, has become increasingly popular over the last 20 years, partly due to the high costs associated with recruitment. It is particularly popular in organisations where jobs are highly sought after. The better assessments include a mix of personality and aptitude questionnaires that are integrated to find the 'best fit for purpose' from the candidates being assessed. Data interpretation comes under the 'ability' category of questionnaires. These instruments are designed to find out what skills employees possess in certain areas, such as data interpretation, and to enable the employer to collect as much evidence as possible on which to base decisions about the candidate. They do not measure general intelligence but do form part of an intelligence quotient (IQ) and although psychologists suggest that IQ is hereditary, it is possible to improve performance through learned behaviours, trends analysis and recognition patterns, and therefore practice can have a favourable impact on performance.

The BPS has two qualification levels, A and B, for test providers. Level A qualifies individuals to provide ability tests including data interpretation and Level B enables the provision of personality questionnaires. All the recognised tests have undergone rigorous studies in reliability and validity resulting in vast statistical sampling. Reliability means that if you retake the same test within a few weeks, the score should not be very different unless the context has changed, for example you have become ill, there has been emotional trauma or you have been practising or had coaching between the two attempts. Validity means that the test really tests what it is designed to test, meaning that it has a focus and the evidence produced by the candidate (you) backs up the focus of areas to be measured.

These tools for measuring our abilities are key to providing objectivity to recruitment and selection processes. Interviewers and selection panels have often been criticised for making subjective decisions, using the 'old boys' network' or some similar derogatory accusation because others have been unable to make sense of the decisions made. Interviews on their own, although having great potential to discover the candidate's capabilities, often do not work because:

- Interviewers are not trained in interview skills.
- There is not enough time to prepare well.
- Decisions are made from limited information about the candidate as it is expensive to spend time on a one-to-one basis discovering competences and capabilities.
- Personal references are often unreliable.
- Interviewing for potential is open to subjectivity and depends on the true understanding of the role and its needs by the interviewer.
- Human beings find it unnatural to have standard interview processes and techniques. We prefer to respond on a case-by-case basis with other individuals.

Psychometrics enable some objectivity to be added to what is a very human process by taking some of the intuition and emotion out of the process through the application of unbiased measures.

Despite some controversial articles in the press expressing concerns about bias against sex and ethnic minorities most candidates feel that psychometric assessments are a way of measuring their skills objectively and fairly. Tests are designed to make fair judgements about individuals. It is illegal to discriminate on grounds of sex, race, disability and age. These variants have been taken into account when designing tests and you will be measured against people with a similar background to yourself or against the general population. These measures are called 'norm groups' which are large statistical samples carried out as part of the test development process to ensure reliability and validity. If you do have any disability that will affect your test performance, for example dyslexia or a physical disability, it is vital you let the test administrator know well in advance so that arrangements can be made for you. If English is not your first language it is possible that you may be able to take the test in your own language – certainly the major test providers, including SHL, are able to offer a multitude of language options.

If you have picked up this book the chances are that you are anticipating some psychometric assessment in the near future. You may be nervous or concerned and this is perfectly normal. You may have specific qualifications and/or skills and the tests will give extra information which enables the employer to identify potential and/or define who will benefit most from a development programme.

This book has been written to help you prepare for the assessment and gain some practice and tips and techniques to enable you to achieve the best results you possibly can. With a little preparation you will be able to improve your score quite dramatically. Peter Rhodes, author of the *Critical Verbal Reasoning* book in this series, offers excellent guidance on the significant improvements that can be made in any psycho-metric test results. According to Peter Rhodes, psychometric tests are based on the assumption that they give only a glimpse or an estimate of someone's 'true score' and that their results are made up of their real level of ability plus some 'junk' factors. 'Junk factors' include anxiety, low expectations of success, lack of confidence, and so on, and these can all get in the way of you doing your best. Unfortunately the scores are treated as if they are straightforwardly 'true' with little account taken of the degree of error they contain.

There are two ways in which the instruments are used:

1 As a stand-alone assessment which allows unfavourable candidates to be filtered out before the interview stage. If you fail this you won't get a chance to put things right at the interview.

2 As part of an overall assessment which includes an interview, other instruments (usually verbal and spatial reasoning) and exercises and can take a day or more to complete.

This book explains the background to assessment, the issues surrounding best practice and confidentiality, and gives you the opportunity to undertake some practice questions and check your results so that you can gain confidence to go and do the real thing. It will help you improve your score by increasing your understanding of how to do well, familiarising you with the levels of sophistication of the questions, helping you understand your response strategy regarding speed versus accuracy, understanding what is required of you and, finally, give you the confidence to ask for a 'test environment' or room that meets your needs regarding adequate heating, ventilation, lighting and freedom from noise and interruptions. Test administrators are duty bound through their professional training to minimise the distractions.

Most psychometric tests measure results in terms of percentiles. These should not be confused with percentages. The term percentile refers to the proportion of the standard group who would achieve the same or a worse score than you. That means that you are on the 45th percentile if 45 per cent of the people have either got the same score or did worse than you and 55 per cent of the comparison group have done better. Peter Rhodes suggests that this gives psychometric tests a spurious air of accuracy that they do not deserve as they massively overstate small differences in scores in the middle of the range (where most of us actually fall).

To illustrate this point, Peter shares some data used to interpret candidates' performance collected by his assessment consultancy, OTL, which is similar to that provided by test publishers to organisations and used to assess the performance of candidates.

Candidates' score	Percentile
39	75
38	70
37	65
36	65
35	45
34	40
33	35
32	30
31	25

In this typical data, only eight scores separate those on the 75th percentile from those on the 25th. The test has 56 questions but as percentiles understate the differences at the extremes, there is only a two percentile difference between those who achieve 44 and those who score 56 (97th and 99th percentiles). This means that all the 'action' in percentile terms is in the middle range. If you score in the centre of the range (where most of us do), it needs only a slight improvement to shift your score, *in percentile terms*, dramatically. For example, only four more questions attempted and answered correctly could take you from the 40th to the 70th percentile in this example. Some results produce even more dramatic increments than this. The more the score is interpreted against 'restricted groups', such as managers or supervisors, the more pronounced the effect is likely to be.

In reality, as Peter Rhodes says, these relatively insignificant differences in scores tend to be overinterpreted in organisational environments. A selection panel would assume that the candidate on the 70th percentile is significantly better than the one on the 40th percentile. In reality the difference could be the result of one candidate making two lucky guesses and the other making two unlucky guesses.

The key point here is that for most of us, a small shift in response rate can have a significant impact on the percentile we achieve therefore the more practice we have, the more confidence we will develop and the more rapidly we can progress through a set of questions.

A word of warning: speed is important but accuracy is even more vital.

The most useful way to use the book is to work through as many of the questions as you choose, then look up the answers and check your reasoning against the explanations in Chapter 3. If your answer is incorrect go back to the question and see if you can work out the reason for your error on your own.

DATA INTERPRETATION INSTRUMENTS

Data interpretation instruments have established a track record in predicting who possesses these skills and at what level. They are traditionally administered towards the end of a recruitment or promotion assessment centre, however increasingly they are being seen as part of an 'e-screening process' via the 'Online Data Interpretation' used through SHL and other psychometric providers. Based on extensive research the assessments use a system of online screening unique to SHL and these instruments are built into the screening process, usually after a biographical or competence sifting, and are accessed by candidates in a controlled environment (a password issued by the professionally trained test administrator). Each candidate accesses a unique instrument. When used in this way, they are marked and in some cases have a cut-off point above which you must pass. Often these tests are timed, with time pressure being a factor for effective performance in the tests.

As well as being used to screen candidates for recruitment, these tests can also be used to check out suitable jobs for people. To quote Gill Hawsley, Commercial HR Manager for Aventis Pharma:

'. . . candidates feel that because they have filled out something objective, they have some "ownership" in the selection process, the company benefits because the profile can support the evidence we see, to give objective feedback. We will also be able to give better feedback, particularly to unsuccessful candidates at assessment centres, stressing their competences. We can discuss the facts objectively and present the future positively. At development centres, the objectivity is helpful when the candidate's own vision of their development does not accord with the evidence gathered. It is important to build the assessment centres carefully to help line managers understand what they need to identify. It's a partnership between HR and the line managers, adding value.'

Data interpretation exercises look at a candidate's ability to understand and manipulate data within relationships and concepts, to demonstrate a mixture of technique and reasoning. In today's complex environment data interpretation is being seen as an increasingly important business skill reaching across all functions and areas of professional expertise.

Many jobs include some form of data analysis and senior managerial roles particularly require role holders to be proficient in financial data analysis, identifying variances and making informed projections for the future. As a candidate these exercises can be helpful in assisting you to display your strengths and contribute towards there being a 'right fit, first time' in your next job. They often allow abilities that have not been brought to the fore during interviews and appraisals to come to light. You may even discover talents you did not know you had.

There are several levels of instrument varying from those used for graduate recruitment, staff who need to show good understanding of data and technique in their jobs, and higher levels for managers who need to understand and marshal data dealing with trends analysis in managing the business environment. Depending on the level and application, candidates may or may not be permitted to use a calculator.

The instruments can be administered using work booklets and answer sheets or a computer display and keyboard. Materials are carefully controlled and not available for prior inspection or practice.

Those administering the assessment will have a manual which has full information on how to administer the instrument and the technical specifications behind it. All of these should have been considered before making the decision to use the specific instrument in the given context. It will have information about the groups of people the instrument was benchmarked against so that your score can be compared with those of similar types of people, for example school leavers, graduates or middle management. The construction of the instrument will have been extremely thorough in order to provide the best possible opportunity to compare your ability with that of others.

Once you have completed your tests it is normal to be offered feedback at a later date and usually over the telephone. If it is not offered you should request feedback.

Test administrators have clear guidelines regarding the storage of tests, so if you are subsequently employed they should be stored in your confidential personnel file and only those trained in interpretation should have access to them, although summaries may be talked through with your line manager. If you are not employed by the company your results should be destroyed.

Before you attempt the practice questions in this book, work through the next few pages (12–20) to familiarise yourself with the varying types of charts and tables used to present data.

Examples of how information may be presented from which to extract data are given below, in the following formats:

- pie chart
- column chart
- line graph
- blocked format line graph

- radar chart
- cylinder chart
- doughnut chart
- tables
- scatter graph.

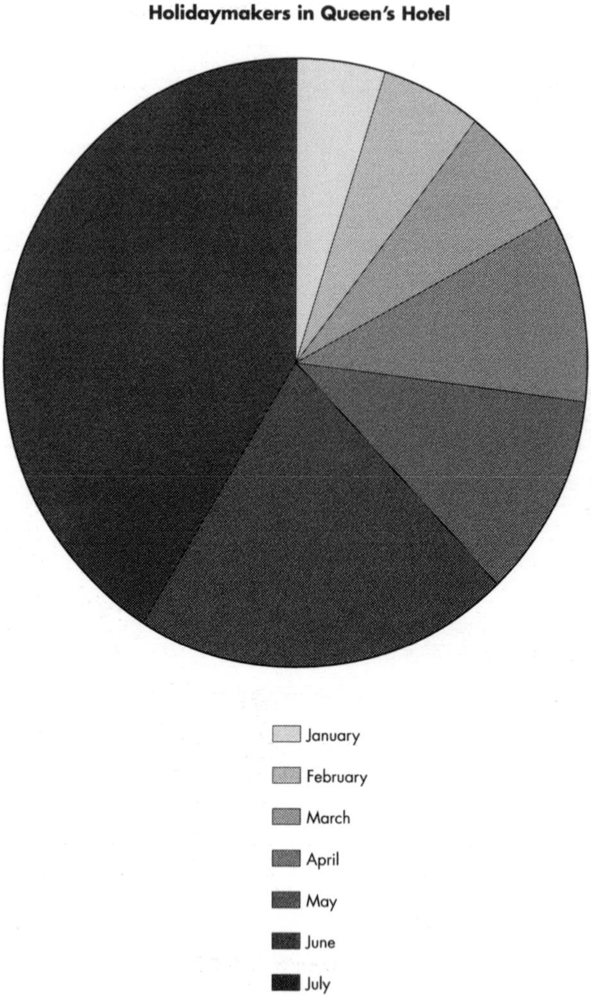

Holidaymakers in Queen's Hotel

January

February

March

April

May

June

July

Figure 1.1 This is known as a pie chart and you could be asked questions regarding the information it shows. For example, which month has the largest number of holidaymakers? The answer is July, which is reached by matching the colour representing the month to the colour of the largest segment.

Holidaymakers in Queen's Hotel

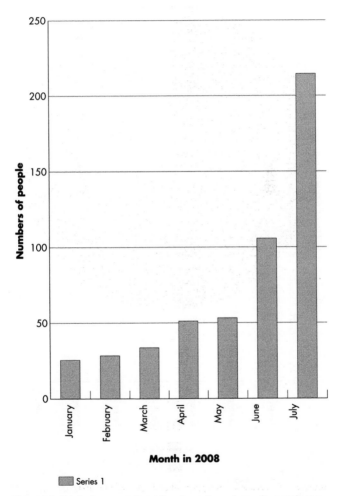

Series 1

Figure 1.2 This is the same information shown in a column chart, and as you can read, July shows the largest number of holidaymakers in the Queen's Hotel.

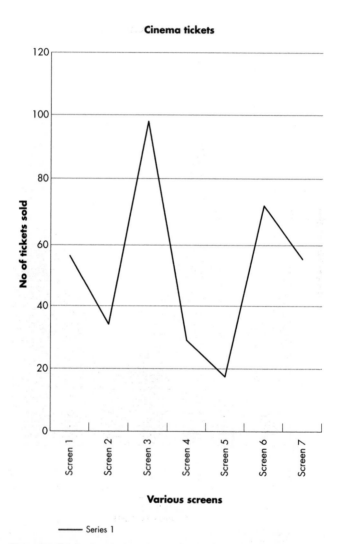

Cinema tickets

Figure 1.3 This line graph shows how many tickets were sold for each screening in a cinema, so if you were asked how many tickets were sold for Screen 3 the answer would be 99.

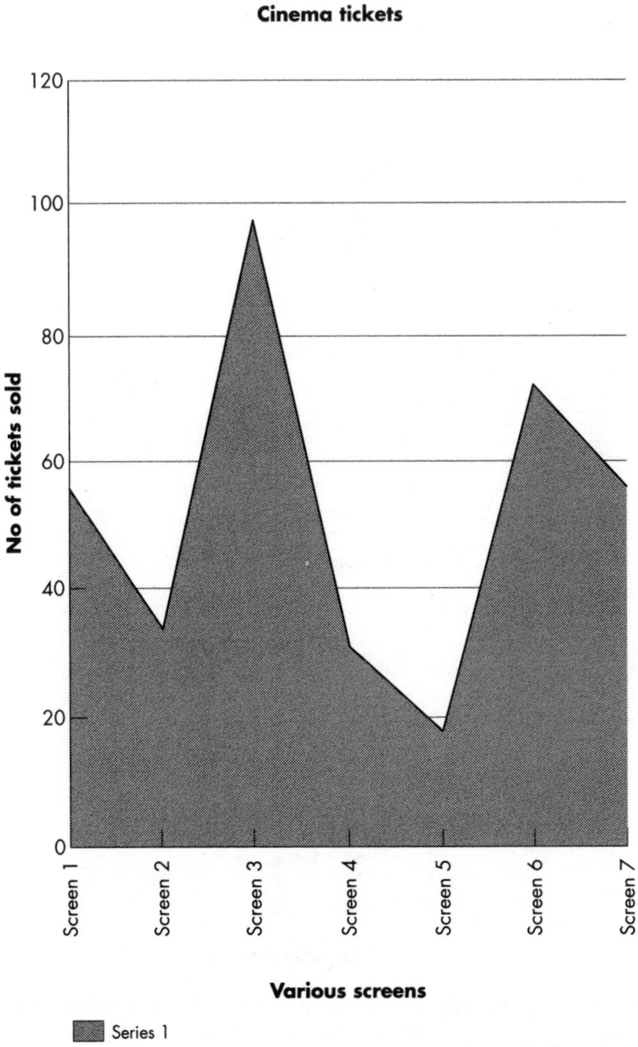

Cinema tickets

Figure 1.4 This area chart shows the same information in a blocked format.

Visitors to fashion shows

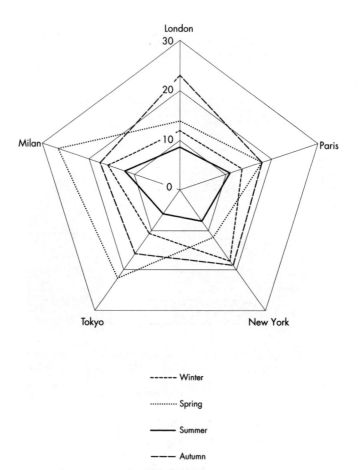

Figure 1.5 This is a radar chart and shows where visitors are most likely to go for fashion shows and when. From this it can be deduced that the most favoured fashion show is in Milan in spring, closely followed by Tokyo, and the least favoured is in summer in Tokyo.

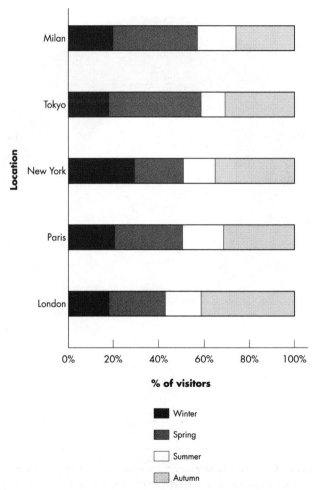

Visitors to fashion shows

Figure 1.6 Here the same information is shown on a cylinder chart. So you can deduce that London has the highest percentage of visitors in the autumn, whereas Tokyo has the lowest in the summer.

Visitors to fashion shows

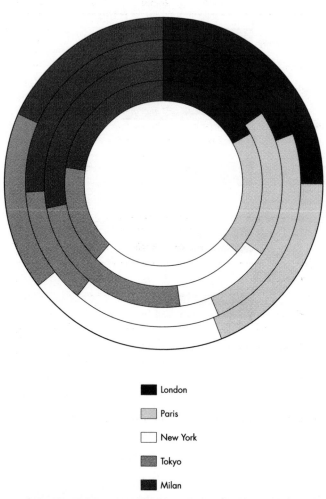

London

Paris

New York

Tokyo

Milan

Figure 1.7 This is the same information as shown in Figures 1.5 and 1.6, but is shown here in a doughnut chart.

Exam pass results for Year 10 pupils by house

	French	English	Maths	Science
Robins	9	16	14	11
Woodpeckers	12	14	12	11
Yellowhammers	15	12	15	16
Blackbirds	14	13	17	21

Figure 1.8 This is a simple table from which it is possible to deduce that more Blackbirds passed Science than any other subject, that Robins appear to be better at English than French, and Woodpeckers are as good at French as they are at Maths.

Exam pass results for Year 10 pupils by house

	French	English	Maths	Science
Robins	9	16	14	11
Woodpeckers	12	14	12	11
Yellowhammers	15	12	15	16
Blackbirds	14	13	17	21

Figure 1.9 A slightly different layout giving the same information.

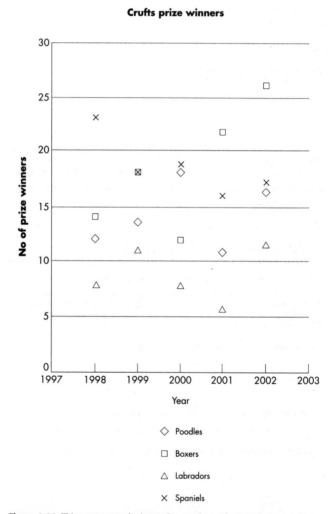

Crufts prize winners

◇ Poodles

□ Boxers

△ Labradors

✕ Spaniels

Figure 1.10 This scatter graph shows the numbers of prize winners and types of dogs winning over a 5-year period at Crufts. It can be deduced that in 2002 Boxers won most prizes while in 2001 Labradors won the least number of prizes.

CHAPTER TWO
TIMED TESTS

It will help you to do well in your tests if you are familiar with the type of questions asked. On the following pages are some practice questions. Guidelines for timing are offered, and for all questions you should work as quickly and accurately as possible because the real instruments may have time limits. These questions are designed to assist you in understanding written information, drawing inferences, interpreting and utilising business related data.

Three golden rules apply to answering the test questions, which are as follows:

- Always work as quickly as possible, and at the same time as accurately as possible.

- Always do as many questions as possible.

- Never spend too much time on any one question – move on to the next one if you are struggling and return to it later if you have time available.

TEST ONE

(Answers to this test can be found on pages 119–123.)

How many questions can you get right in 45 minutes?

QUESTION ONE

An insurance scheme pays benefits to its members who are sick for extended periods at the following rates:

1st month nil

2nd–4th months 50 per cent of normal pay

5th and successive months 25 per cent of normal pay

on the first £24,000 p.a. of the salary for each month in which the member is sick and is not paid by the employer. How much does the scheme pay to:

1   John, who is off work for two months, whose salary is £12,000 p.a. and who gets no sick pay.

2   Pat, who is ill for six months, but who is paid normally for the first two months and whose salary is £18,000 p.a.

3   Hilary, whose salary is £30,000 p.a., who gets 3 months' sick pay from her employer and takes 9 months off.

a	£250	b	£500	c	£750	d	£1000
e	£1125	f	£1500	g	£1765	h	£2125
i	£2250	j	£2350	k	£2500	l	£3125
m	£3750	n	£4000	o	£5000	p	£5625

QUESTION TWO

Television viewing habits: 250 people were asked what sort of TV programme they liked the most.

Age	11–15	16–20	21–25
Cartoons	24%	15%	4%
Feature films	20%	23%	20%
News	5%	18%	21%
Soaps	15%	20%	20%
TV Dramas	8%	10%	13%
Sports	18%	14%	22%
Number in survey	**120**	**80**	**50**

1 Over all ages what is the most popular sort of TV programme?

a Sports

b Soaps

c Feature films

d Cartoons

e News

2 What proportion of 16–20-year-olds watch something other than the News?

a 54%

b 18%

c 28%

d 82%

e 74%

3 What sort of programme shows the greatest increase as viewers get older?

a News

b TV Dramas

c Soaps

d Sports

e cannot tell

4 How many 16–20-year-olds like cartoons the most?

a 15

b 10

c 8

d 12

e 16

5 How many more 11–15-year-olds like to watch feature films compared with 21–25-year-olds?

a 14

b 10

c 8

d 12

e 16

6 What sort of programme do 11–15-year-olds spend the most time watching?

a Cartoons

b Feature films

c Soaps

d News

e cannot tell

QUESTION THREE

Burger meals: A burger chain reported the following sales of $\frac{1}{4}$ pounders and $\frac{1}{2}$ pounders.

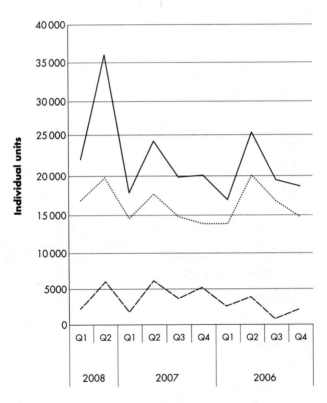

Burger production

Quarterly total

—— Production

······ 1/4 pounders

– – 1/2 pounders

1 How many burgers were produced and not sold in Q3 2007?

a 7000

b 20,000

c 1000

d cannot say

2 Which quarter of the year appears consistently busier in terms of sales?

a Q1

b Q2

c Q3

d Q4

3 If the difference between sales and production is wastage, when was the highest period of wastage?

a Q1 2007

b Q2 2006

c Q3 2006

d Q2 2008

4 What was the total number of burgers sold in 2007?

a 17,500

b 62,000

c 79,500

d cannot say

5 In Q2 2006 what percentage of total production were $\frac{1}{4}$ pounders?

a 20%

b 80%

c 75%

d cannot say

QUESTION FOUR

Absence records: an organisation recorded the following absenteeism.

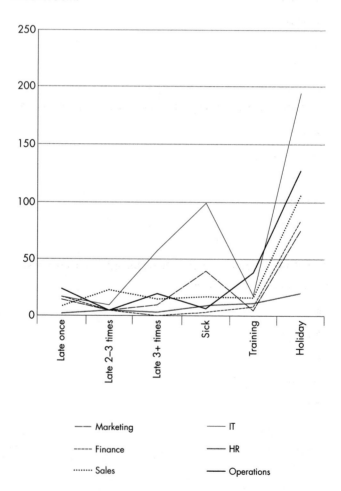

1 Which department employs the most people?

a Marketing

b Finance

c Sales

d IT

e cannot say

2 Which department takes the most holiday per employee?

a IT

b Operations

c Sales

d Finance

e cannot say

3 If IT use 60 more sick days than Marketing, how many sick days do Marketing use?

a 40

b cannot say

c 51

d 100

e 45

4 Which department takes least time out of the business?

a Operations

b Sales

c Finance

d HR

e IT

5 What is the lowest overall reason for absence?

a Late 2–3 times

b Sickness

c Training

d Late 3+ times

QUESTION FIVE

Clothes returns: a department store made an analysis of returns of female garments

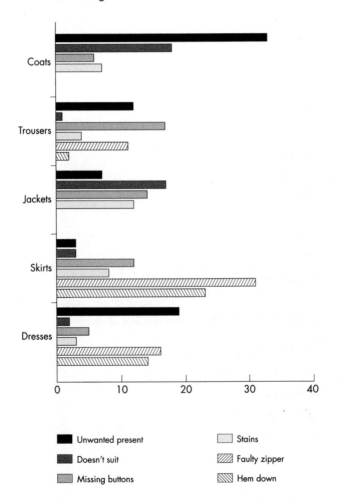

1 If most presents are bought by partners, which garment do partners prefer to give as gifts?

a coats

b skirts

c dresses

d jackets

e cannot say

2 If all skirts with missing buttons also have faulty zippers, what is the total of skirts with zipper and/or button problems?

a 43

b 31

c 19

d 12

e cannot say

3 Which item has the largest number of returns?

a coats

b skirts

c dresses

d trousers

e cannot say

4 Which is the most frequent reason for returned garments?

a doesn't suit

b unwanted present

c faulty zipper

d cannot say

5 Which garments do not get returned for having hems down?

a coats

b skirts

c skirts and trousers

d coats and jackets

QUESTION SIX

Analysis of school entrants in 2007.

Name of school	Girls	Boys	Total
St James'	21	33	54
St John's	25	27	52
Petworth	11	19	30
Lady Mary	14	27	41
Hillview	0	19	19
Treetops	32	33	65
Hillside	28	36	64
Totals	**131**	**194**	**325**

1 Which school accepts only boys?

a Hillside

b St James'

c St John's

d Hillview

e cannot say

2 What percentage of girls attend Treetops?

a 28%

b 24%

c 32%

d 25%

e cannot say

3 What is the total number of new girls and boys at St John's and Hillside?

a 53

b 63

c 116

d 325

e cannot say

4 What percentage of total school entrants are girls?

a 60%

b 40%

c 33%

d 41%

e cannot say

5 Which pair of schools has the most new entrants?

a St John's / Petworth

b Treetops / Hillview

c Hillside / Petworth

d St James' / Lady Mary

QUESTION SEVEN

Sales trends of replacement windows and doors.

	Quarter 1	Quarter 2	Quarter 3	Quarter 4
Sash windows	16	24	24	16
Full pane	11	19	3	21
French doors	7	7	14	21
Patio doors	9	27	45	63
Totals	**43**	**77**	**86**	**121**

1 What percentage of total sales are patio doors in Quarter 3?

a 53%

b 45%

c 52%

d 86%

e cannot say

2 If the trend for French doors continues, how many will be sold in the next quarter?

a 21

b 14

c 28

d 42

e cannot say

3 If every full pane window is sold with a patio door in Quarter 4, how many patio doors were sold on their own?

a 21

b 63

c 42

d 84

e cannot say

4 What is the total number of doors and windows, excluding full pane windows, sold during the year?

a 100

b 121

c 273

d 237

e cannot say

5 What are total sales of replacement windows for Quarter 1 as a percentage of total sales for the year?

a 15%

b 22%

c 35%

d 8%

e cannot say

QUESTION EIGHT

Library records: books borrowed by 8-year-olds.

	2006	2007	2008
Fiction %	77.2	74.4	82.3
Animal stories %	*32.1*	*33.4*	*35.6*
Mysteries %	*35.5*	*34.2*	*36.1*
Fairy tales %	*9.6*	*6.8*	*10.6*
Language books %	9.1	12.9	11.6
Others %	13.7	12.7	6.1
Total number of books borrowed	**1816**	**1972**	**1987**

1 How many more fiction books were borrowed in 2008 than 2006?

a 1402

b 1635

c 171

d 233

e 243

2 What is the total number of animal story books borrowed over the 3 years?

a 583

b 1949

c 1963

d 707

e cannot say

3 What percentage of books borrowed in 2007 were language books?

a 12.7

b 12.9

c 11.6

d 9.1

e cannot say

4 How many books, other than fiction and language, were borrowed in 2007?

a 121

b 1756

c 250

d 248

e cannot say

5 What percentage of animal stories and mysteries were borrowed in 2006?

a 77.2

b 13.7

c 67.6

d 65.5

e 69

6 What percentage more books were borrowed in 2008 than in 2006?

a 17.1

b 8.6

c 9.4

d cannot say

e 10%

7 How many fairy tale books were borrowed in 2007?

a 174

b 230

c 134

d 183

e cannot say

QUESTION NINE

Nationality: cross section of course delegates.

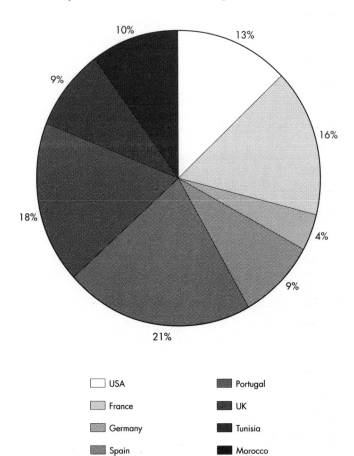

1 What percentage of delegates are Moroccan?

a 9%

b 10%

c 13%

d 9%

e cannot say

2 What percentage of delegates speak English as a first language?

a 18%

b cannot say

c 31%

d 13%

e 15.5%

3 If the total number of delegates is 11,654, how many are from Portugal?

a 1865

b 1846

c 2474

d 2447

e cannot say

4 If 50% of the Portuguese and 30% of the French are male and the rest of the delegates are female, what percentage of the whole are female?

a 84%

b 82%

c 85%

d 63%

e 98%

5 What percentage of total delegates is European?

a cannot say

b 87

c 81

d 68

e 43

6 If the total number of delegates is 1326, how many are from Germany and Spain?

a 53

b 119

c 172

d 132

e cannot say

QUESTION TEN

Restaurant customer feedback.

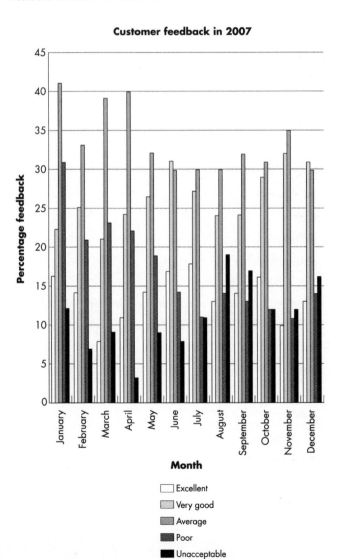

Customer feedback in 2007

1 In which month did the highest percentage of customers
   give excellent feedback?

a January

b June

c July

d October

e April

2 When did customers find service most unacceptable?

a April

b February

c June

d December

e August

3 If the total number of customers in January was 100, how
   many gave excellent feedback?

a 41

b 84

c 16

d 41

e cannot say

4 If the total number of customers in December was 650, how many gave poor feedback?

a 140

b 14

c cannot say

d 589

e 91

5 If exactly the same 100 customers came in both April and May, how many more of them found the service unacceptable in May?

a 9

b 3

c cannot say

d 6

e 12

6 If exactly the same number of customers came in both January and July, how many of them changed their opinion in July from average to something else?

a 11

b 71

c 21

d 41

e cannot say

QUESTION ELEVEN

Narrow boat owners in Europe by country.

	English	French	German	Spanish	Italian
2005	168	219	425	116	317
2006	114	272	312	119	109
2007	143	294	398	267	297

1 Which country has owned the least number of boats over the 3-year period?

a England

b Spain

c Italy

d Portugal

e cannot say

2 If England had sold 50% of her boats to Spain in 2006, what percentage of the total boats for that year would Germany have owned?

a 7%

b 10%

c 30%

d 33%

e cannot say

3 If Italy bought 40% of France's boats in 2005, how many would Italy have had?

a 448

b 317

c 405

d 636

e cannot say

4 If all English boats originated in Spain, what percentage of the Spanish boats have been sold to England over the 3-year period?

a 64%

b 33%

c 53%

d 46%

e cannot say

5 If 10% of English boats came from Italy and 24% came from Spain, how many boats originated in England?

a 280

b 66%

c 144

d 110

e cannot say

TEST TWO

(Answers to this test can be found on pages 123–125.)

How many questions can you get right in 40 minutes?

QUESTION TWELVE

Simple profit and loss account over 3 years for XYZ Engineering Ltd

	2005	2006	2007
Revenue			
Gross revenue	1278	1369	
(VAT)	190	208	
Net revenue	**1088**	**1161**	**1235**
Cost of sales			
Raw materials	329	360	349
Direct labour	100	112	151
Consumables	115	176	132
Total cost of sales	**544**	**648**	**632**
Operating costs			
Salaries and wages	87	110	
Staff training	19	21	23
Marketing	64	64	
Product development	20	17	26
Professional fees	10	10	10
Staff subsistence	3	4	6
IT	13	13	12
Telephones	20	14	17
Total operating costs	**236**	**253**	**295**
Fixed costs			
Serviced premises	100	125	125
Franchise fee	108	116	123
Total fixed costs	**208**	**241**	**248**
Trading profit	**100**	**19**	**60**

1 What is the gross revenue for 2007?

a 1235

b 1460

c 1245

d 1451

e cannot say

2 Salaries and wages are increased by 12.5% per annum. What is the figure for 2007?

a 125.75

b 127

c 123.75

d 125

e 112.5

3 How much was spent on Marketing in 2007?

a 64

b 70

c 77.25

d 65

e cannot say

4 What is the trading profit in 2006 as a percentage of net revenue?

a 1.4

b 14

c 1.6

d 16

e cannot say

5 What is the net revenue increase in 2007 as a percentage against net revenue in 2005?

a 10.7

b 11.9

c 6.2

d 13.5

e 6.4

6 In 2007 what was the total of all costs?

a 927

b 543

c 1175

d 880

e cannot say

7 In 2006 what was the cost of sales as a percentage of net revenue?

a 50%

b 49%

c 56%

d 47%

e 44%

8 What percentage of net revenue for the 3 years is staff training?

a .02%

b 2%

c 20%

d 12%

e cannot say

QUESTION THIRTEEN

Teaching qualifications by subject.

Teaching qualifications

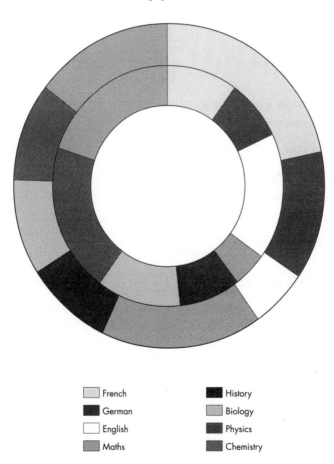

☐ French		■ History	
■ German		▨ Biology	
☐ English		■ Physics	
▨ Maths		▨ Chemistry	

1 Which subject has the largest number of qualified teachers?

a French

b German

c Chemistry

d Physics

e cannot say

2 Which subject has the lowest number of qualified teachers?

a Maths

b History

c German

d Biology

e cannot say

3 Which subject has the third largest number of qualified teachers?

a French

b Chemistry

c German

d Physics

e cannot say

QUESTION FOURTEEN

Sales of Christmas decorations: these are only on sale in the last quarter of each year.

Year	Month	Direct sales	Online sales	Returns
2005	October	26000	17000	6500
	November	54000	23658	14871
	December	13000	4320	2116
2006	October	28450	18234	1581
	November	65152	27971	16320
	December	12176	6789	1889
2007	October	32124	19056	14000
	November	78142	17683	11297
	December	16578	9004	2342

1 What was the total number of sales in the last quarter of 2006?

a 18,965

b 105,778

c 52,993

d 158,772

e cannot say

2 How many more direct sales than online sales were made over the 3 years?

a 325,622

b 143,715

c 181,907

d 469,337

e cannot say

3 What was the final number of sales over the 3 years after returns had been made?

a 325,622

b 143,717

c 398,421

d 469,337

e cannot say

4 What was the percentage increase in direct sales in 2007 against 2005?

a 48%

b 36%

c 46%

d 45%

e cannot say

5 How do returns in 2006 compare with returns in 2005?

a 16% increase

b 84% decrease

c 16% decrease

d cannot say

6 Which month of which year was the most successful taking all sales and returns into account?

a Nov 2006

b Dec 2007

c Nov 2007

d Oct 2006

e Oct 2007

7 How do online sales for November 2007 compare with online sales for November 2006?

a 37% increase

b 63% decrease

c 63% increase

d 37% decrease

e cannot say

QUESTION FIFTEEN

Ice cream: sales by flavour.

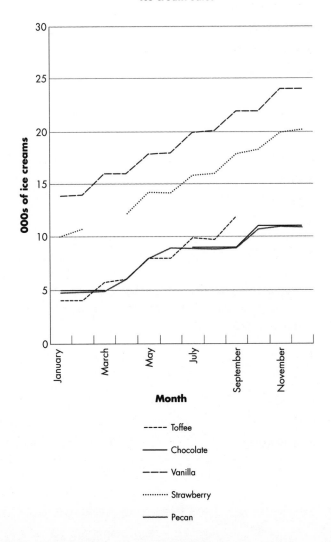

Ice cream sales

1 What are the total sales of toffee ice cream for October, November and December (in 000s)?

a 36

b 44

c 32

d 40

e cannot say

2 What are the total sales of pecan ice cream for April, May and June (in 000s)?

a 15

b 23

c 21

d 26

e cannot say

3 What are the total sales of strawberry ice cream for February and March if the trend stays the same over the year (in 000s)?

a 22

b 24

c 20

d 21

e cannot say

4 What are the total ice cream sales for October (in 000s)?

a 74

b 76

c 78

d 80

e cannot say

5 If the trends shown continue what will be the sales of ice cream in January and February of the following year (in 000s)?

a 93

b 177

c 186

d 187

e cannot say

TEST THREE

(Answers to this test can be found on pages 125–129.)

How many questions can you get right in 70 minutes?

QUESTION A

This question consists of a series of instructions, followed by a number of questions. You are asked to use the instructions to answer the questions, which follow. Then circle the appropriate letter **a**, **b**, **c**, **d** or **e** for each question.

You are carrying out a computer check of personnel records. Which codes should be used to show the following records?

> If the staff member has left the organisation enter code L alone into the computer. For all staff members still present code P together with the appropriate check code below.
>
> If the home address has changed enter code A; otherwise enter code B. If the home telephone number has changed enter code T. If the home telephone number is the same enter code C.
>
> If the name of the staff member's Doctor has changed enter code D; otherwise enter code N. If the Doctor's telephone number has changed enter code R. If the telephone number is the same enter code S.
>
> Code letters are to be entered in the sequence given above.

1 Employee number 1 is still a staff member. His address has changed but he has kept the same telephone number. There is no change to his Doctor's details.

a PANS

b ACNS

c PACNS

d PANCS

e PACSN

2 Employee number 2 changed her Doctor a year ago but in the past month has left the organisation.

a LR

b LNR

c RL

d L

e LRN

3 Employee number 3 is still a staff member. His address and telephone number are the same and so is the name of his Doctor. However his Doctor is operating from a different address and telephone number.

a PBCR

b PBCRN

c PCN

d LPBCR

e PBCNR

4 Employee number 4 is still a staff member. Her address and telephone number are unchanged. Her Doctor's name and telephone number are unchanged.

a PBN

b PBCNS

c PNSBC

d PACNS

e PBTNS

QUESTION B

This test, comprising two graphs, looks at your ability to understand graphs and statistical tables and to draw appropriate conclusions from them. You will be using facts and figures presented in various ways to answer a range of questions. In each question you are given five answers to choose from. One and only one of the answers is correct in each case.

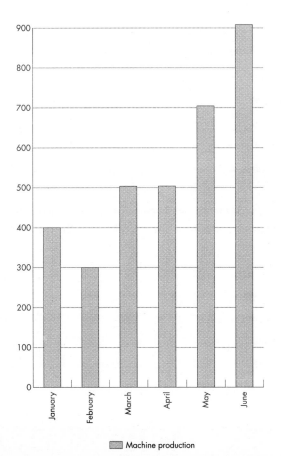

Machine production

1 How many machines were produced in the first 3 months of the period?

a 900

b 1000

c 1100

d 1200

e none of these

2 If the trend of the last 3 months continues, how many machines will be produced in July?

a 1100

b 1200

c 1300

d 1400

e cannot say

3 In which month did machine production figures show the greatest percentage change, relative to the previous month?

a February

b March

c April

d May

e June

MAGAZINE READERSHIP

Magazine title	Estimated numbers of readers (in millions)		Percentages of copies sold in 1993 by outlet	
	1983	1993	Subscription	Newsagents
Home Hints	4.8	2.4	47%	13%
Business Tomorrow	1.1	1.4	58%	24%
Computer News	2.3	4.6	34%	24%
Travel Plus	8.5	6.1	25%	44%
Leisure Time	7.5	8.0	28%	47%

4 What was the combined readership of Home Hints, Travel Plus and Leisure Time in 1983 (in millions)?

a 7.2

b 16.5

c 20.8

d 37.3

e none of these

5 What percentage of copies of Computer News were sold in specialist computer shops in 1993?

a 24%

b 34%

c 42%

d 66%

e cannot say

6 If 1.0 million copies of Travel Plus were sold by subscription, how many copies were sold overall in 1993 (in millions)?

a 1

b 2.9

c 4

d 6.1

e 8.5

QUESTION C

In this section you will need to refer to a timetable and a route map in order to answer questions, each of which takes the form of a passenger enquiry. For each question you are given the name of the station, where you are and the current time. This information will be different in each question so you must check it carefully.

For each question you must decide which of the five answers given is the correct answer to the enquiry and mark the appropriate circle **a**, **b**, **c**, **d** or **e**. Now work through the three questions below using the timetable and route map.

TIMETABLE

Milson Line							
Brook Road	1730	1745	1755	1802	1805	1811	1815
Appletree Farm	1735	1750	1800	1807	1810	1816	1820
Queen's Junction	1739	1754	1804	1811	1814	1820	1824
The Dales	1742	1757	1807	1814	1817	1823	1827
Sinclair Road	1747	1802	1812	1819	1822	1828	1832
Mill Rise	1751	1806	1816	1823	1826	1832	1836

ROUTE MAP

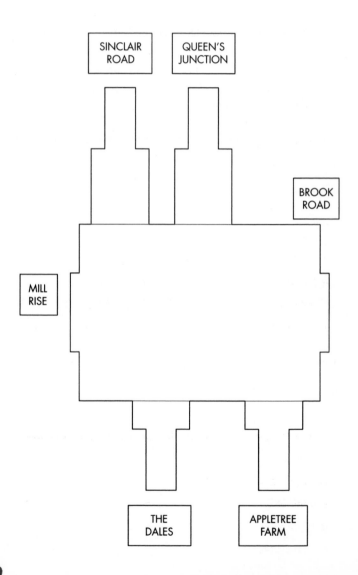

1 Station: Brook Road

Time: 1735

When is the next train to Appletree Farm?

a 1737

b 1740

c 1745

d 1750

e 1755

2 Station: Queen's Junction

Time: 1811

How long does the train take to reach Sinclair Road?

a 3 minutes

b 5 minutes

c 6 minutes

d 7 minutes

e 8 minutes

3 Station: Appletree Farm

Time: 1745

How long do I have to wait for the next train to Mill Rise?

a 5 minutes

b 7 minutes

c 9 minutes

d 10 minutes

e 12 minutes

QUESTION D

In this test, in four parts, you are asked to use facts and figures presented in statistical tables to answer the questions below. In each question you are given options from which to choose. One and only one is the correct answer in each case.

POPULATION STRUCTURE 1985

	Population at start of year in millions	Live births per 1000 population Jan–Dec	Deaths per 1000 population Jan–Dec	% of population under 15 at start of year	% of population aged 60 or over at start of year
UK	56.6	13.3	11.8	19	21
France	55.2	13.9	10.0	21	19
Italy	57.1	10.1	9.5	19	19
Germany	61.0	9.6	11.5	15	20
Spain	38.6	12.1	7.7	23	17

1 Which country had the highest number of people aged 60 or over at the start of 1985?

a UK

b France

c Italy

d Germany

e Spain

2 How many live births occurred in 1985 in Spain and Italy together (to the nearest 1000)?

a 104,000

b 840,000

c 1,044,000

d 8,400,000

e 10,440,000

3 What was the net effect on the UK population of the live birth and death rates in 1985?

a −66,700

b +84,900

c +85,270

d +752,780

e cannot say

PRODUCTION OF 15MM BUTTONS JULY–DECEMBER

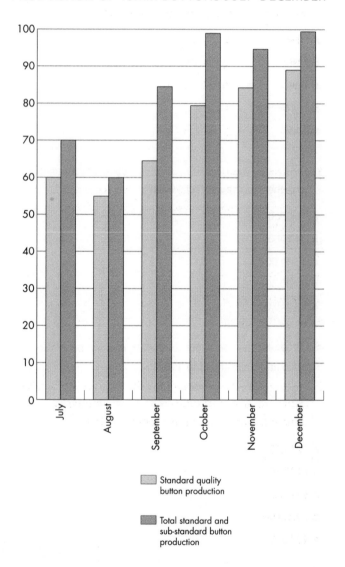

Standard quality
button production

Total standard and
sub-standard button
production

1 What percentage of the total 15mm button production was classed as sub-standard in September?

a 10.5%   **f** 25%

b 13%   **g** 23.5%

c 15%   **h** 27.5%

d 17.5%   **i** 28%

e 20%   **j** 30.5%

2 Assume standard buttons cost £5.70 per 100 and sub-standard buttons half of that. By how much did the total sales value of November's button production vary from October's?

a £28.50 decrease

b £142.50 decrease

c £285.00 increase

d £427.50 decrease

e no change

3 What was the loss in potential sales revenue attributable to the production of sub-standard (as opposed to standard) buttons over the 6-month period?

a £213.75

b £427.50

c £2137.50

d £2280.00

e 4275.00

HORSERACING

Racehorses	Bets in £millions in 1989	Bets in 1990	% of males betting on each horse in 1990	% of females betting on each horse in 1990
Red Star	3.6	2.9	7	6
Night Rider	13.8	9.3	24	18
Dream Journey	1.1	1.4	4	3
Deb's Delight	8.5	12.7	30	23
Dawn Raider	4.8	4.9	10	12

1 Which horse was backed by a higher percentage of females than males in 1990?

a Dream Journey

b Deb's Delight

c Night Rider

d Dawn Raider

e Red Star

2 What were the combined bets on Red Star, Dream Journey and Dawn Raider in 1989 (in £millions)?

a 10.6

b 8.4

c 9.5

d 12.2

e 7.8

3 Which racehorse showed the largest change in female betting between 1989 and 1990?

a Dawn Raider

b Dream Journey

c Deb's Delight

d Red Star

e cannot say

AMOUNT IN MILLIONS OF DOLLARS SPENT ON COMPUTER IMPORTS

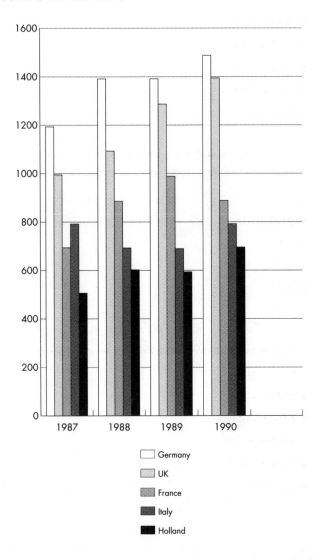

1 In 1989 how much more than Italy did Germany spend on computer imports?

a $650 million

b $700 million

c $750 million

d $800 million

e $850 million

2 If the amount spent on computer imports to the UK in 1991 was 20% lower than in 1990, what was spent in 1991 (in $millions)?

a 1080

b 1120

c 1160

d 1220

e 1300

3 Which countries experienced a drop in the value of computers imported from one year to the next?

a France & Italy

b France & Holland

c Holland & Italy

d UK & Holland

e Italy & UK

QUESTION E

These questions are advanced managerial questions aimed at graduates and those applying for middle to senior management positions. How many can you answer in 10 minutes?

STAFF PROFILE, YEAR 1

Function

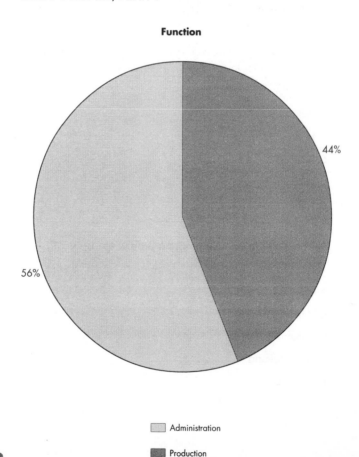

44%

56%

Administration

Production

Length of service in years

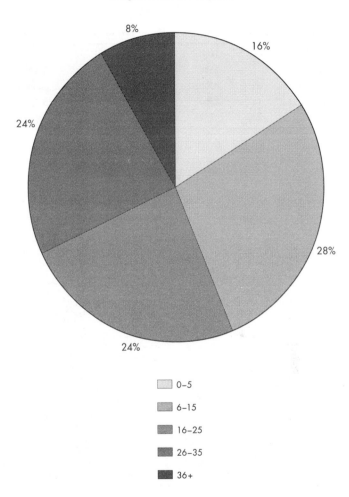

8%
16%
24%
28%
24%

- 0–5
- 6–15
- 16–25
- 26–35
- 36+

Total number of staff = 275

SALES FIGURES – YEARS 1 TO 3

Sales (£000s)

Product group	Year 1	Year 2	Year 3
A	1420	1560	1610
B	2670	2940	2880
C	4100	3690	3140
D	2360	2830	3120
E	930	1040	860

SALES DEPARTMENT – STAFF NUMBERS, YEARS 1 TO 3

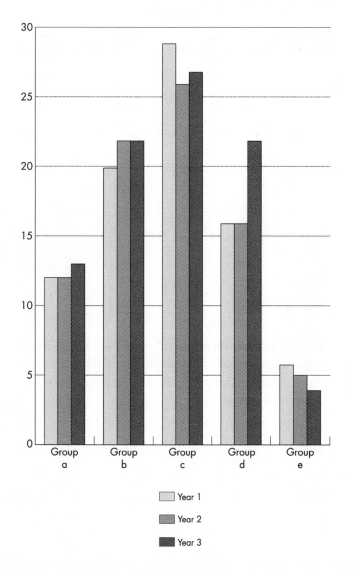

1 How many more production staff are there than administrative staff?

a 12

b 27

c 33

d 110

e cannot say

2 How many administrative staff have served between 10 to 20 years?

a 31

b 57

c 72

d 89

e cannot say

3 How many administrative staff are there in the 26–35 years' service group, if the proportion of production staff and administrative staff is the same for this group as for the overall group?

a 11

b 29

c 37

d 49

e 52

4 If half of the 0–5 years' service group and all of the 36+ years' service group are production staff, how many production staff are there altogether in the other groups?

a 110

b 132

c 164

d 231

e cannot say

5 By what percentage did total sales staff numbers change from Year 1 to Year 3?

a 2.4%

b 3.5%

c 4.8%

d 6.0%

e 9.4%

6 Which product group achieved the best sales result per sales person in Year 2?

a Group a

b Group b

c Group c

d Group d

e Group e

7 Which product group's sales figures for Years 1 to 3 show the closest trend to its sales staff numbers over the same period?

a Group a

b Group b

c Group c

d Group d

e Group e

8 If there were seven additional sales staff in Year 3, and the average sales per person remained constant, how much greater would the total sales for Year 3 be?

a £12,500

b £855,500

c £923,500

d £1,253,400

e cannot say

QUESTION F

This section consists of a number of statistical tables displaying various facts and figures to which you need to refer in order to answer the questions. How many can you answer in 15 minutes?

CEMENT PRODUCTION, DELIVERY AND IMPORTS (000s OF TONNES)

Date	Quarter	Production	Deliveries	Imports
2008	Q1	2786	2781	307
	Q2	3122	3014	290
2007	Q1	3016	2976	357
	Q2	3369	3120	382
	Q3	3242	3097	349
	Q4	2845	2661	312
	Total	**12474**	**11754**	**1400**
2006	Q1	2918	2814	228
	Q2	3331	3062	235
	Q3	3364	3108	278
	Q4	3084	2752	408
	Total	**12697**	**11736**	**1149**

1 How many more tonnes of cement were produced than delivered in the first quarter of 2007 (in thousands of tonnes)?

a 5

b 40

c 104

d 249

e cannot say

2 What percentage of the total imported cement in 2006 was imported in the third quarter?

a 19.8%

b 20.4%

c 24.2%

d 35.5%

e cannot say

3 How does cement production in 2008 compare with that in 2007?

a decrease by 47%

b decrease by 7.5%

c increase by 7.5%

d increase by 47%

e cannot say

PARTICIPATION IN EDUCATION AND TRAINING OF 16-YEAR-OLDS

	2005	2006	2007
Full time education (%)	69.4	69.8	71.2
Maintained schools (%)	*28.0*	*28.2*	*28.5*
Independent schools (%)	*6.4*	*6.3*	*6.2*
Further education (%)	*35.0*	*35.3*	*36.4*
Other education and training (%)	17.2	16.8	15.5
Not in any education or training (%)	14.2	14.2	14.0
Number of 16-year-olds (thousands)	610.00	600.4	609.1

4 In 2006, approximately how many 16-year-olds were not in any full-time education or training?

a 45,250

b 50,550

c 62,000

d 85,250

e none of these

5 How many more 16-year-olds were there in full-time education in 2007, compared with 2006?

a 160

b 1460

c 1600

d 14,600

e 16,000

6 In 2005, approximately what proportion of 16-year-olds in full-time education were in independent schools?

a 6%

b 9%

c 11%

d 14%

e 19%

7 Which type(s) of full-time education showed a year-on-year decrease in the proportion of 16-year-old students between 2005 and 2007?

a maintained schools

b independent schools

c further education

d all of them

e none of them

DRIVING TEST APPLICATIONS AND RESULTS (IN THOUSANDS OF APPLICANTS)

	2006	2007
Applications received	1607.9	1631.4
Tests conducted	1482.9	1489.0
Tests passed	697.4	684.2

8 Approximately what percentage of applications received in 2006 resulted in tests being conducted?

a 84%

b 87%

c 92%

d 95%

e 97%

9 How many more tests were failed in 2007 than 2006?

a 1930

b 2010

c 15,700

d 19,300

e 20,100

10 By approximately what percentage did the number of applications received in 2007 increase from the previous year?

  a 1.5%

  b 3.2%

  c 4.7%

  d 10.1%

  e 11.5%

11 If the pass rate falls by 1% per year between 2007 and 2011, how many passes will there be in 2011?

  a 62,380

  b 65,720

  c 623,800

  d 657,200

  e cannot say

EMISSIONS OF CARBON DIOXIDE BY SOURCE (IN MILLIONS OF TONNES)

	1995–97	1998–2000
Industrial combustion	111	108
Power stations	162	132
Transport	105	108
Domestic	72	69
Other sources	33	36

12 What was the total number of tonnes of carbon dioxide emitted by power stations between 1995 and 2000?

a 2,650,000

b 2,940,000

c 3,890,000

d 265,000,000

e 294,000,000

13 What was the approximate change in total carbon dioxide emissions between 1995–97 and 1998–2000?

a decrease by 6%

b decrease by 5%

c decrease by 2%

d increase by 4%

e increase by 5%

14 If the proportion of carbon dioxide emissions from domestic sources decreased by 10% in 2001–3, what would be the total number of tonnes emitted from domestic sources in 2001–3?

a 39,000,000

b 46,000,000

c 52,000,000

d 64,000,000

e 62,100,000

15 In 1998–2000, approximately what proportion of carbon dioxide emissions were from industrial combustion and power stations combined?

  a 48%

  b 53%

  c 57%

  d 67%

  e 80%

16 If emissions from power stations decrease by 10% in each of the following four 3-year periods, what will they be in 2010–12?

  a 71,800,000

  b 79,200,000

  c 86,600,000

  d 94,000,000

  e cannot say

TEST FOUR

(Answers to this test can be found on pages 129–130.)

How many questions can you get right in 15 minutes?

These questions are typical of graduate intake and junior middle management positions.

Mark your answers on the answer sheet at the end of the questions. We suggest you photocopy it for ease of working and so as not to deface the book. You will have 15 minutes to answer the 12 questions. You are allowed to use a calculator, although one is not required. You should use a pencil so you can erase to change an answer.

Every question has five possible answers from which you must choose the most correct answer. You will simply mark *one* of the five answers which will be labelled A, B, C, D, E by shading the appropriate oval shape on the question sheet, as below

1

During an actual test, you will mark your answers on a special answer sheet separate from the questions.

If you mark more than one answer to a question, it will *not* be counted as correct.

If you change your answer, it is important to erase your first answer so it does not appear that you have marked more than one answer.

Each correct answer adds one point to your score. Points are *not* taken off if you mark an incorrect answer. You should try to score as many points as you can.

AMOUNT OF INCOME IN CERTAIN INDUSTRIES (IN BILLIONS OF DOLLARS)

Industry	Year 1	Year 2	Year 3	Year 4	Year 5
Agriculture	22	26	26	30	51
Communication	14	17	18	20	21
Construction	36	43	47	52	57
Finance and Real Estate	78	90	100	108	118
Manufacturing	213	218	226	253	287
Transportation	27	30	33	36	40

1 Which industry had the largest increase in the dollar amount of income from Year 1 to Year 2?

a Agriculture

b Construction

c Finance and Real Estate

d Manufacturing

e Transportation

2 Which industry had the smallest increase in the dollar amount of income from Year 1 to Year 5?

a Agriculture

b Construction

c Finance and Real Estate

d Manufacturing

e Transportation

3 Which industry experienced the largest percentage increase from Year 3 to Year 4?

a Agriculture

b Communication

c Construction

d Finance and Real Estate

e Manufacturing

4 Which industry experienced the least per cent change from Year 1 to Year 4?

a Agriculture

b Communication

c Construction

d Manufacturing

e Transportation

5 For which industry was there the least consistent increase in income over the period of time covered by the table?

a Agriculture

b Construction

c Finance and Real Estate

d Manufacturing

e Transportation

6 If the trend in the Transportation industry were to continue, its income for Year 6 would most likely be about . . .

a 42 billion dollars

b 44 billion dollars

c 46 billion dollars

d 48 billion dollars

e 50 billion dollars

7 In which of the following instances has the first type of industry named consistently had an income about half that of the second?

a Agriculture; Finance and Real Estate

b Communication; Agriculture

c Construction; Finance and Real Estate

d Finance and Real Estate; Manufacturing

e Transportation; Communication

8 In how many instances did a type of industry make a gain of 10% or more over the previous year listed?

a 1–4

b 5–8

c 9–12

d 13–16

e 17–20

9 The type of industry showing the steadiest rate of growth in income during this period was . . .?

a Communication

b Construction

c Finance and Real Estate

d Manufacturing

e Transportation

10 In which one of the following groups did all three types of industry increase their respective incomes by most nearly one-third from Year 1 to Year 3?

   a Agriculture; Communication; Transportation

   b Agriculture; Communication; Construction

   c Communication; Construction; Transportation

   d Construction; Finance and Real Estate, Transportation

   e Communication; Construction; Finance and Real Estate

11 How many industries had a growth rate of at least 20% from Year 1 to Year 3?

   a 1

   b 2

   c 3

   d 4

   e 5

12 Among the following, the greatest percentage increase in income occurred for

   a Agriculture between Year 3 and Year 4

   b Communication between Year 2 and Year 3

   c Construction between Year 1 and Year 2

   d Finance and Real Estate between Year 4 and Year 5

   e Manufacturing between Year 3 and Year 4

ANSWER SHEET FOR THE PROCTER AND GAMBLE QUESTIONS

1   (A)   (B)   (C)   (D)   (E)

2   (A)   (B)   (C)   (D)   (E)

3   (A)   (B)   (C)   (D)   (E)

4   (A)   (B)   (C)   (D)   (E)

5   (A)   (B)   (C)   (D)   (E)

6   (A)   (B)   (C)   (D)   (E)

7   (A)   (B)   (C)   (D)   (E)

8   (A)   (B)   (C)   (D)   (E)

9   (A)   (B)   (C)   (D)   (E)

10 (A)   (B)   (C)   (D)   (E)

11 (A)   (B)   (C)   (D)   (E)

12 (A)   (B)   (C)   (D)   (E)

TEST FIVE

(Answers to this test can be found on pages 130–133.)

This is the type of test often used for people applying for roles where multiple decisions have to be made very quickly from different types of data (e.g. the police, financial trading floors, broadcasting, etc.).

How many of these questions can you answer correctly in 20 minutes? Circle the correct answer.

QUESTION ONE

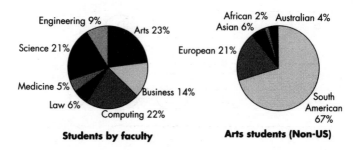

Students by faculty

Arts students (Non-US)

The pie charts above show the percentage of students in each faculty at North West University and the number of non-US students in the Arts Faculty. These percentages have been rounded to the nearest whole number. There are a total of 1049 students in the Arts Faculty. Use this information to answer the following questions.

1 What percentage of students in the Arts Faculty are non-US students?

A	B	C	D	E
14%	9%	30%	11%	15%

2 How many students are there in the Engineering Faculty?

A	B	C	D	E
420	410	390	440	400

3 How many students are there at the University?

A	B	C	D	E
4650	4560	4640	4450	4460

4 If 6 percent of the Science students are Asian, how many Asian students are there studying Science?

A	B	C	D	E
48	66	120	57	43

5 There are 34 European medical students. What percentage of the faculty does this represent?

A	B	C	D	E
14%	18%	12%	16%	15%

QUESTION TWO

Age	15–20	21–30	31+
France	6	4	17
Spain	7	5	5
Tenerife	6	12	14
USA	1	4	11
India	2	3	15
Australia	9	3	4
Thailand	2	2	2
Total	**33**	**33**	**68**

The table above shows a group of people who completed a questionnaire about their holiday destination preferences. Please use the information in the table to answer the following questions.

1 What percentage of people under 31 said that India was their preferred holiday destination?

A	B	C	D	E
7.1	7.6	8.3	14.1	7.2

2 What percentage of people aged 21–30 had a preference other than Tenerife?

A	B	C	D	E
64	60	75	36	46

3 What percentage of the whole group said that the USA is their preferred destination?

A	B	C	D	E
6	8	25	4	11

4 What percentage of the total group is aged 21–30?

A	B	C	D	E
31	23	22	14	30

QUESTION THREE

Town	Jul	Aug	Sep	Oct	Nov	Dec	Total
Bath	680	940	900	1080	1120	1200	5920
Chester	800	880	720	940	940	920	5200
Oxford	740	640	640	640	680	660	4000
York	280	280	280	280	340	280	1740
Cambridge	580	580	560	620	580	620	3540
Sheffield	440	480	480	520	500	460	2880
Total	**3520**	**3800**	**3580**	**4080**	**4160**	**4140**	**23280**

This chart shows the sales of electric bread makers in UK towns and cities in the run up to Christmas. Use the information in the chart to answer the following questions.

1 What percentage of the overall sales was sold in Bath?

A	B	C	D	E
22	25.4	25.8	24.1	24.6

2 What percentage of the overall total was sold in November?

A	B	C	D	E
24.1	25.6	27.1	17.9	20.3

3 Which month showed the biggest increase in sales from the previous month?

A	B	C	D	E
Aug	Sep	Oct	Nov	Dec

4 What percentage of the monthly total was sold to the city with the highest level of sales in August?

A	B	C	D	E
24.7	23.1	36.5	51.1	15.1

5 What is the average number of bread makers per month sold in Sheffield from July to October inclusive?

A	B	C	D	E
440	460	480	500	520

6 What percentage of total bread makers is sold by the three lower selling towns and cities?

A	B	C	D	E
37.1	14.8	40	36.6	35.1

QUESTION FOUR

This chart shows the number of people who have died in ABS Nursing Home over a 6-year period.

	2000	2001	2002	2003	2004	2005
90						
80						▲
70					▼▲	◄
60					■	►■
50		▼◄		▲◄	►◄	▼
40		▲■	▼►◄	▼■		
30	▼◄►	►	▲	►		
20	▲■					
10						
0	2000	2001	2002	2003	2004	2005

▲ = Heart attack
► = Stroke
▼ = Cancer
◄ = Traffic accident
■ = Drug overdose

1 How many people died in 2003?

A	B	C	D	E	F
110	120	170	210	220	260

2 In what year did most people die?

A	B	C	D	E	F
2000	2004	2003	2002	2005	2006

3 How many people in total died of traffic accidents?

A	B	C	D	E	F
210	220	230	240	260	290

4 In what years were there more heart attacks than strokes?

A	B	C	D	E	F
2000	2004	2003	2002	2005	2006

5 Which was the third highest category of deaths?

A	B	C	D	E
Heart attack	Stroke	Cancer	Traffic accident	Drug overdose

6 How many more deaths were there in 2004 than 2001?

A	B	C	D	E
110	90	0	80	20

CHAPTER THREE
ANSWERS TO AND EXPLANATIONS OF TIMED TESTS

TEST ONE

QUESTION ONE

1 **b**

2 **i**

3 **n**

In this example the scheme only comes into effect once the employee's sick pay stops. Reading the information given will help you answer the questions correctly.

QUESTION TWO

1 **c** Feature films because they are all 20% plus

2 **d** 100% − 18% = 82%

3 **a** News goes from 5% to 21%

4 **d** 15% of 80 = 12

5 **a** (20% of 120) − (20% of 50) = 14

6 **e** cannot tell, there is no information on the length of the programmes

QUESTION THREE

1 **d** there is no information as to what else was produced

2 **b** Q2 total sales are higher in each year, add together the $\frac{1}{4}$ pounder and $\frac{1}{2}$ pounder results

3 **d** Q2 2008, 36,000 − 26,000 = 10,000

4 **d** cannot say, we don't know if the difference is waste or sales

5 **b** 80%, 20,000 expressed as a percentage of 25,000 is 80%

QUESTION FOUR

1 **e** cannot say, no total number of employees

2 **e** not enough information

3 **a** 100 − 60 = 40

4 **d** HR is consistently low across the bottom of the graph

5 **a** late 2–3 times, look for the lowest scores over all departments – the troughs on the chart

QUESTION FIVE

1 **e** not enough information about total sales of presents

2 **b** 31, those with missing buttons are included in those with faulty zippers

3 **b** skirts, 80 of them

4 **b** there are 74 unwanted presents overall

5 **d** coats and jackets, neither have any recorded returns for hems down

QUESTION SIX

1 **e** cannot say, there is no evidence that Hillview doesn't take girls, only that there were no new girls in 2007

2 **b** 24%, 32 expressed as a percentage of 131

3 **c** 116, total of 52 at St John's and 64 at Hillside

4 **b** 40%, 131 as a percentage of 325

5 **d** St James' and Lady Mary, add together the totals of each from the totals column to get 95 which is the highest total of any pair

QUESTION SEVEN

1 **c** 52%, 45 expressed as a percentage of 86

2 **c** 28, trend has increased by 7 per quarter over the last three quarters

3 **c** 42, $63 - 21 = 42$

4 **c** 273, total of the four quarters minus the full panes in each quarter

5 **d** 8%, $16 + 11 = 27$ (column one) as a percentage of the totals 327 $(43 + 77 + 86 + 121) = 8\%$

QUESTION EIGHT

1 **d** 233, 82.3% of 1987 − 77.2% of 1816

2 **b** 1949, 32.1% of 1816 + 33.4% of 1972 + 35.6% of 1987

3 **b** 12.9, read across the table from 'language books' to '2007' column

4 **c** 250, 12.7% of 1972

5 c 67.6, add 32.1 + 35.5

6 c 9.4%, the difference between 1987 and 1816 = 171 expressed as a percentage of 1816

7 c 134, 6.8% of 1972

QUESTION NINE

1 b 10%, match the country code to the segment of the pie chart

2 c 31%, total of UK and USA

3 d 2447, 21% of 11,654

4 a 84%, 100% − 5 (30% of 16) − 10.5 (50% of 21) rounded up = 84%

5 d 68%, 100% – USA, Tunisia and Morocco

6 c 172, Germany and Spain = 13%, 13% of 1326 is 172

QUESTION TEN

1 c July, look for the highest column with the excellent code, which represents the highest number of customers giving excellent feedback

2 e August, look for the code for unacceptable and then the highest column in that code and read down to get the month

3 c 16, read the first column in January across to the % axis

4 e 91, 14% of 650

5 d the difference between 3 in April and 9 in May

6 e cannot say, we do not know how many customers came, only the percentages (read the question carefully)

QUESTION ELEVEN

1 a England, add the columns down and Portugal is not featured

2 d 33%, 312 expressed as a percentage of 926. Spain is a red herring

3 c 405, 40% of 219 + 317, then rounded up

4 d 46%, add all the English and Spanish boats and express the total English as a percentage of that total

5 d cannot say, no information as to where the rest came from

TEST TWO

QUESTION TWELVE

1 d 1451, 117.5% of 1235

2 c 123.75, 110 + 12.5% is 123.75

3 d 65, relies on getting question 2 right, add all costs and take from total costs of 295 to get missing figure

4 c 1.6, 19 expressed as a percentage of 1161

5 d 13.5, 1235 − 1088 = 147 then express as a percentage of 1088

6 c 1175, add up the cost of sales, operating costs and fixed costs

7 c 56%, express 648 as a percentage of 1161

8 b 2%, 63 as a percentage of 3484

QUESTION THIRTEEN

1 **c** Chemistry, the code for this subject covers the largest area

2 **b** History, the code for this subject covers the smallest area

3 **d** Physics, the code for this subject covers less area than Chemistry and slightly less than French

QUESTION FOURTEEN

1 **d** 158,772, add all the direct and online sales for October, November and December 2006

2 **c** 181,907, total the direct sales and online sales

3 **c** 398,421, total all sales minus total of all returns

4 **b** 36%, add up 3 months' direct sales for 2007, take off 3 months' direct sales for 2005 and express the difference as a percentage of 93,000

5 **c** 16% decrease, total returns for 2005 less total returns for 2006 and express as a percentage of 2005

6 **c** November 2007, total direct sales and online sales minus total returns for that month is 84,528

7 **d** 37% decrease, the difference between 27,971 and 17,683 expressed as a percentage of 27,971

QUESTION FIFTEEN

1 **d** 40, sales increase by 2 in alternate months so will be 12, 14, 14 for these months

2 **c** 21, sales increase by 2 each quarter so 7,7,7, is the trend for these 3 months

3 a 22, strawberry sales increase by 2 in alternate months so 10 + 12 = 22

4 b 76, if we follow the trend for October and total that column, the total is 76

5 d 187, project the trends for each flavour forward by two months and then total

TEST THREE

The SHL questions.

QUESTION A

1 c staff member, new address, same phone number, same Doctor with same phone number and in the sequence requested

2 d left and no other codings apply

3 e staff member and all the same except the Doctor and in the sequence requested

4 b still a staff member and no changes, in the sequence requested

QUESTION B

1 d 400 + 300 + 500 = total of Jan–March from bar chart readings

2 a increase of 200 machines per month

3 b 200 machines was a 66% increase over the 300 in Feb, the increases of 200 machines in May and June did not give such great percentages over the previous months

4 **c** $4.8 + 8.5 + 7.5 = 20.8$

5 **e** we have no information regarding specialist computer shops

6 **c** if a million = 25% then 100% must be 4 million ($4 \times 25\%$)

QUESTION C

1 **c** you have just missed the 1730 so following the timetable along to the next column, the next train at Brook Road is 1745

2 **e** the 1811 at Queen's Junction will arrive at Sinclair Road at 1819, a difference and therefore a journey of 8 minutes

3 **a** the next train comes at 1750 so you will have to wait for 5 minutes

QUESTION D

POPULATION

1 **d** Germany, 20% of 61 million is greater than 21% of 56.6 million

2 **c** $12.1 \times 1000 \times 38.6 + 10.1 \times 1000 \times 57.1$

3 **b** remember to multiply out the percentages by 1000 and by the population at the start of the year

BUTTONS

1 **g** 85,000 produced, 65,000 were standard therefore 20,000 sub-standard which is 23.5% of the total

2 **e** there was no change. By multiplying out the sales figures you will see that the differences between standard and sub-standard compensate for each other

3 **c** add up the total production for the 6 months and cost it at £5.70 per 100, then add up the sub-standard production and multiply by £2.85 (the difference between £5.70 and £2.85) and take this away from the first total

HORSERACING

1 **d** Dawn Raider, 12% is higher than 10%

2 **c** 3.6 + 4.8 + 1.1 = 9.5

3 **e** cannot say, we do not have figures for females in 1989

COMPUTERS

1 **b** follow the graph up from 1989, Italy spent $700m and Germany spent $1400m, making a difference of $700m

2 **b** the UK spent $1400m in 1990, 20% is $280 making a reduction to $1120m

3 **a** look at the graph and notice which countries had readings of a lower value than a previous year – Italy from 1987 to 1988 and France from 1989 to 1990

QUESTION E

1 **c** there are 12% more production staff than administrative and 12% of the total of 275 is 33

2 **e** cannot say as the pie chart does not distinguish between the two functions

3 b 24% of the total of 275 is 66 and 44% of 66 is 29

4 a 8% plus half of 16% is 16%. 56% of the whole are production staff so if 16% are accounted for that leaves 40% of 275 in the other groups, i.e. 110

5 d total for Year 1 is 83, total for Year 3 is 88. The difference of 5 is 6% of 83

6 e five people achieved sales of £1040, i.e. £208 per head

7 d sales figures and staff numbers have increased year on year

8 c if 88 staff can sell £11,610 (total sales for Year 3) then the average sale, multiplied by 95 staff gives a difference between the two totals of £923,500

QUESTION F

1 b the difference between 3016 and 2976

2 c add up the imports for 2006 and express 278 as a percentage of the total

3 e not enough information as two quarters of 2008 are missing

4 d 14.2% of 600.4

5 d the difference between 71.2% of 609.1 and 69.8% of 600.4

6 b express 6.4 as a percentage of 69.4

7 b read across from the school in italics and see that independent schools decreased each year

8 c in the 2006 column express 1482.9 as a percentage of 1607.9

9 d subtract the tests passed from the tests conducted for each year then subtract the 2006 result from the 2007 result

10 a in the applications received row subtract 1607.9 from 1631.4 and express the difference as a percentage of 1607.9

11 d take 1% of 684.2 to get the rate for 2008, then repeat for each year taking 1% from each reduced total until you get to 2011

12 e read across from power stations and add the two figures for each set of years together

13 a add all the figures together to get a total for each 3-year period and express the difference as a percentage of the 1995–97 total

14 e 69 minus 10% is 62.1, multiply by 1,000,000

15 b add together the figures for industrial combustion and power stations for 1998–2000 and express as a percentage of the total emissions for that 3-year period

16 c take the total emissions for 1998–2000, reduce by 10% to get a lower result, then repeat with each lower total four times to get the answer

TEST FOUR

The Procter and Gamble questions

1 c there is a difference of 12 between Year 1 and Year 2

2 e work out the differences between the years and total them

3 **a** work out the differences between Years 3 and 4 and express as a percentage of Year 3. The answer is that which reflects the greater difference

4 **d** work out the differences between Years 1–4 for each industry, total them and express as percentages of the totalled changes

5 **a** look for the trends in the differences year on year

6 **b** there is a pattern of increase of 10% year on year so $40 + 4 = 44$

7 **c** look for the pattern of the first industry being approximately 50% of the second one year on year

8 **d** review the differences year on year in each column for each industry and total the differences

9 **e** a difference of 10% year on year is the highest growth

10 **e** take the totals of Year 1 and increase them by a third. Compare your findings to the Year 3 totals to get your answer

11 **c** as question 10 but look to increase by one-fifth

12 **c** look to see where the major difference is between the years

TEST FIVE

QUESTION ONE

1 **d** the total of all categories of non-US students = 112 which is 11% of 1049; ensure you read the whole question very carefully

2 **b** we know that 9% of the students are Engineering and that 1049 Arts students = 23% so divide 1049 by 23 to get 1% and multiply by 9 to get the number of Engineering students

3 **b** from the previous question we know that 1% of students = 45.6 so multiply by 100% to get the total number of students

4 **d** again we know that 1% is 45.6 so we multiply that by 21 to get a total number of 958 Science students, then calculate 6% of 958 to get the number of Asian Science students

5 **e** we now know that there are 4560 students at the University and 5% of them are studying Medicine, so work out 5% which is 228 and represent the 34 European students as a percentage of 228 to get your answer

QUESTION TWO

1 **b** the total number of respondents under 31 is 66, and the total number of respondents under 31 who prefer India is 5 so you need to express 5 as a percentage of 66

2 **a** we know the total number of repondents under 31 is 66, so take away the total of 18 who prefer Tenerife to leave 48, then express 48 as a percentage of 66

3 **e** add up the total respondents to get 134, then add up the total who prefer the USA = 16 and express 16 as a percentage of 101

4 **c** we now know there are 134 respondents in total, so express 33 as a percentage of 134

QUESTION THREE

1 **b** take the overall number of total sales in Bath and express as a percentage of the total sales of 23280

2 **d** take the total of 4160 and express as a percentage of 23280

3 **c** read the totals column and look for the high sales numbers, then look at the previous month's numbers and choose the pair with the largest difference

4 **a** read the August column and note that Bath sold the most with 940 sales, then express 940 as a percentage of 3800 which are the total sales in August.

5 **c** take the total Sheffield sales for July–October which is 1920 and divide by 4 to get 480

6 **e** the three smallest are York, Cambridge and Sheffield, so add together their total sales and express as a percentage of the total 23280

QUESTION FOUR

These answers rely on checking the symbols very accurately.

1 **d** all five symbols are represented in the column so add up $2 \times 50 + 2 \times 40 + 30$ to get the correct answer

2 **e** look for the symbols at the higher end of the x axis

3 **f** check out the symbol for road traffic accidents, but be careful not to confuse it with the symbol for drug overdose and read off the corresponding numbers for each year then add them together

4 **b,c,e**, note the symbols and that in each year except 2000 and 2002 they were the same or heart attacks were higher

5 **c** scan for the three symbols which occur most frequently towards the higher value top of the chart and add up the three, taking the lower result as your answer

6 **b** read off the values for each symbol by year for 2004 and 2001 and subtract the 2001 total from the 2004 total; ensure you read all the symbols in each column

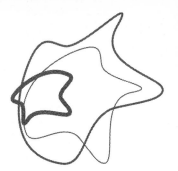

CHAPTER FOUR
DIAGNOSIS AND
FURTHER READING

DIAGNOSIS

Each psychometric test has its own scoring system. There is no pattern and no way of predicting what it can be. Some questionnaires award extra points for attempting all the questions, some deduct points for wrong answers, some questions have different points allocation from others.

What is common is that your score will be rated against a 'norm' group of similar people to yourself, for example school leavers, graduates or middle managers. There may also be norms for particular functions or specialisms such as engineers or clerical workers.

Some tests are scored in terms of percentiles, not to be confused with percentages. A percentile represents the number of people in the 'norm' group who do worse than the candidate. So the 40th percentile means that 40 per cent of the group would do worse than the candidate and 60 per cent would do better. For example, for a senior manager in the UK any percentile between 16th and 84th could be considered typical for a job at this level. Percentiles are widely used, however they do cause problems by exaggerating the differences between candidates in the middle of the range. They also underestimate the differences between candidates who have high or low scores. They may be difficult to add up, weight or average out as required at assessment centres. It is important here to remember or re-read what was described in Chapter One, where we explained that for most of us, a small shift in response rate can have a significant impact on the percentile we achieve, therefore the more practice we have, the more confidence we will develop and the more rapidly we can progress through a set of questions.

It is therefore useful for the assessor to use Standard Scores which can be added or weighted to give an overall performance across all tests. An average manager achieves a Standard Score of between 40 and 60 on each test. The total Standard Score should be between 80 and 120 and a middle range candidate will score 100. This provides the interview panel with a quick and easy estimate of the candidate's overall ability.

When scores are different enough to be able to discount the possibility that the difference is spurious (caused by lucky or unlucky guesses) then a line is drawn under the candidate's name. Where the scores are different but not different enough to make a legally defensible claim that one candidate is better than another then no line is drawn.

Tests are not perfect. The best and worst scores provide an indication of how a candidate's performance may vary if he or she were to do the test again. The effects of the time of day, nerves and lucky/unlucky guesses are built into these figures. In other words, even allowing for these factors, the best the candidate can be expected to do is often quoted alongside the most pessimistic estimate of his/her ability – thus giving a range rather than a defined score. If you feel that you did not do your best, that you found the questions or language of the questions difficult, it is worth mentioning this at interview providing it is in a non-defensive and collaborative way with some balanced evidence as to what you found difficult and what worked really well for you. Do not use this discussion as a way of justifying the findings, merely as a pointer if you truly believe you could have done better.

The world of psychometric testing is growing, and especially the sphere of data interpretation. With the numerous vocational, modular, sandwich and flexible degree courses now available, employers find it difficult to be fully aware of the content of previous learning. Testing, especially computerised testing, is becoming more popular. Coupled with this, the emerging importance of work–life balance, anti-stress campaigns, and interest in whole life development, employees will no longer stay in a job in a company and/or culture they cannot endure. These tests assist in that filtering process and so if the results are not favourable, rather than feel rejected the candidate should view the feedback in a positive and developmental manner and should take the opportunity to gain some free career consulting by asking questions about the positive trends from the feedback and suitability for other areas of work.

Giving feedback can be time consuming, however an ethical test administrator will want to help and may offer the feedback over the telephone. Those running assessment centres or recruitment agencies carrying out testing on behalf of a client will be more likely to give face-to-face feedback and in fact often wish to do so as the following conversations can prove enlightening and add great value to the process. If you feel you have not performed as well as you could have done, this is a great second opportunity for you to prove your ability.

Whatever happens, reflect on the feedback you receive, it could alter your perception of your own abilities and have a profound impact on your career plans. Go away and practise those areas where your performance has been weaker.

SUGGESTIONS FOR FURTHER IMPROVEMENT

Recent research has indicated that the following practices can lead to better scores on data interpretation questionnaires, including some you *should* do, and some you should *not* do.

BEFORE YOUR TEST

Get as much practice as you can at working through questions and ensure you understand what is required by reading books such as this.

What you *should* do to score well on a data interpretation questionnaire:

- Determine clearly the nature of the question before looking at the answer choices.
- Scan the whole graph or table before you start answering the questions.
- Make sure you know what each figure reflects, e.g. measurements of money, quantity, or other units.

- Work as fast as possible with reasonable assurance of accuracy: do not lose time on a question you do not understand.
- Keep your rough workings as once you have worked out an answer you may need it again further on in the question.
- Eliminate answers from consideration that you know are incorrect and choose from among the remaining answers.
- Mark an answer to every question.
- Beware of your brain racing ahead and making patterns. Sometimes a trick question will catch you out by not asking the most obvious question.
- Use any time remaining after completion of the test to reconsider your answers.

What you should *not* do when answering a data interpretation questionnaire:

- Do not read slowly and carefully through the entire test before you start working. It's only worth working on one question at a time.
- Do not spend time verifying questions you have already answered until you have answered every question.
- Do not spend time considering an answer that is *not* one of the answer choices. The answer will be given, although there may be red herrings.

ON THE DAY

You must plan to arrive at the test centre in a state that is conducive to achieving your best possible score. This means being calm and focused. It is possible that you may feel nervous before the test, but you can help yourself by preparing in advance the practical details that will enable you to do well. Remember, it is unlikely that you are the only person who is feeling nervous; what is important is how you deal with your nerves! The following suggestions may help you to overcome unnecessary test-related anxiety.

1 Know where the test centre is located, and estimate how long it will take you to get there – plan your 'setting off time'. Now plan to leave 45 minutes before your setting off time to allow for travel delays. This way, you can be more or less certain that you will arrive at the test centre in good time. If, for any reason, you think you will miss the start of the session, call the administrator to ask for instructions.

2 Try to get a good night's sleep before the test. This is obvious advice and, realistically, it is not always possible, particularly if you are prone to nerves the night before a test. However, you can take some positive steps to help. Consider taking a hot bath before you go to bed, drinking herbal rather than caffeinated tea, and doing some exercise. Think back to what worked last time you took an exam and try to replicate the scenario.

3 The night before the test, organise everything that you need to take with you. This includes test instructions, directions, your identification, pens, erasers, possibly your calculator (with new batteries in it), reading glasses, and contact lenses.

4 Decide what you are going to wear and have your clothes ready the night before. Be prepared for the test centre to be unusually hot or cold, and dress in layers so that you can regulate the climate yourself. If your test will be

preceded or followed by an interview, make sure you dress accordingly for the interview which is likely to be a more formal event than the test itself.

5 Eat breakfast! Even if you usually skip breakfast, you should consider that insufficient sugar levels affect your concentration and that a healthy breakfast might help you to concentrate, especially towards the end of the test when you are likely to be tired.

6 If you know that you have specific or exceptional requirements which will require preparation on the day, be sure to inform the test administrators in advance so that they can assist you as necessary. This may include wheelchair access, the availability of the test in Braille, or a facility for those with hearing difficulties. Similarly, if you are feeling unusually unwell on the day of the test, make sure that the test administrator is aware of it.

7 If, when you read the test instructions, there is something you don't understand, ask for clarification from the administrator. The time given to you to read the instructions may or may not be limited but, within the allowed time, you can usually ask questions. Don't assume that you have understood the instructions if, at first glance, they appear to be similar to the instructions for the practice tests.

8 Don't read through all the questions before you start. This simply wastes time. Start with Question 1 and work swiftly and methodically through each question in order. Unless you are taking a computerised test where the level of difficulty of the next question depends on you correctly answering the previous question (such as the GMAT or GRE), don't waste time on questions that you know require

a lot of time. You can return to these questions at the end if you have time left over.

9 After you have taken the test, find out the mechanism for feedback, and approximately the number of days you will have to wait to find out your results. Ask whether there is scope for objective feedback on your performance for your future reference.

10 Celebrate that you have finished.

So, in conclusion, you might be dreading data interpretation tests, but do not worry since these tests really are something you can prepare for and subsequently improve your test score. It is amazing how many people still think that you can't improve your score in aptitude tests through practising. The limiting belief that you have to be a very clever person to pass these tests with a high mark still prevails for some reason. This is not true and you will be surprised at what kinds of improvements you can achieve by taking the time to practise and develop your own strategy for success. Practice really does make a difference.

FURTHER SOURCES OF PRACTICE

In this final section, you will find a list of useful sources for all types of psychometric tests.

BOOKS

Bolles, Richard N., *What Color Is Your Parachute?* Berkeley, CA: Ten Speed Press, 2007.

Carter, P. and K. Russell, *Psychometric Testing: 1000 Ways to Assess Your Personality, Creativity, Intelligence and Lateral Thinking.* Chichester: John Wiley, 2001.

Jackson, Tom, *The Perfect Résumé*. New York: Broadway Books, 2004.

Kourdi, Jeremy, *Succeed at Psychometric Testing: Practice Tests for Verbal Reasoning Advanced*. London: Hodder Education, 2008.

Krannich, Ronald L. and Caryl Rae Krannich, *Network Your Way to Job and Career Success*. Manassa, VA: Impact Publications, 1989.

Nuga, Simbo, *Succeed at Psychometric Testing: Practice Tests for Verbal Reasoning Intermediate*. London: Hodder Education, 2008.

Rhodes, Peter, *Succeed at Psychometric Testing: Practice Tests for Critical Verbal Reasoning*. London: Hodder Education, 2008.

Rhodes, Peter, *Succeed at Psychometric Testing: Practice Tests for Diagrammatic and Abstract Reasoning*. London: Hodder Education, 2008.

Walmsley, Bernice, *Succeed at Psychometric Testing: Practice Tests for Numerical Reasoning Advanced*. London: Hodder Education, 2008.

Walmsley, Bernice, *Succeed at Psychometric Testing: Practice Tests for Numerical Reasoning Intermediate*. London: Hodder Education, 2008.

Walmsley, Bernice, *Succeed at Psychometric Testing: Practice Tests for the National Police Selection Process*. London: Hodder Education, 2008.

TEST PUBLISHERS AND SUPPLIERS

ASE
Chiswick Centre
414 Chiswick High Road
London W4 5TF
telephone: 0208 996 3337
www.ase-solutions.co.uk

Oxford Psychologists Press
Elsfield Hall
15–17 Elsfield Way
Oxford OX2 8EP
telephone: 01865 404500
www.opp.co.uk

Psytech International Ltd
The Grange
Church Road
Pulloxhill
Bedfordshire MK45 5HE
telephone: 01525 720003
www.psytech.co.uk

SHL
The Pavilion
1 Atwell Place
Thames Ditton
Surrey KT7 0SR
telephone: 0208 398 4170
www.shl.com

The Psychological Corporation
Harcourt Assessment
Halley Court
Jordan Hill
Oxford OX2 8EJ
www.tpc-international.com

The Test Agency Ltd
Burgner House
4630 Kingsgate
Oxford Business Park South
Oxford OX4 2SU
telephone: 01865 402900
www.testagency.com

OTHER USEFUL WEBSITES

Websites are prone to change, but the following are correct at the time of going to press.

www.careerpsychologycentre.com

www.cipd.org.uk

www.deloitte.co.uk/index.asp

www.ets.org

www.freesat1prep.com

www.mensa.org.uk

www.morrisby.co.uk

www.newmonday.co.uk

www.oneclickhr.com

www.pgcareers.com/apply/how/recruitment.asp

www.psychtesting.org.uk

www.psychtests.com

www.publicjobs.gov.ie

www.puzz.com

www.testagency.co.uk

www.tests-direct.com

OTHER USEFUL ORGANISATIONS

American Psychological Association Testing and Assessment – www.apa.org/science/testing

Association of Recognised English Language Schools (ARELS) – www.englishuk.com

Australian Psychological Society – www.psychology.org.au

The Best Practice Club – www.bpclub.com

The British Psychological Society – www.bps.org.uk

Canadian Psychological Association – www.cpa.ca

The Chartered Institute of Marketing – www.cim.co.uk

The Chartered Institute of Personnel and Development – www.cipd.co.uk

The Chartered Management Institute – www.managers.org.uk

Psyconsult – www.psyconsult.co.uk

Singapore Psychological Society – www.singaporepsychologicalsociety.co.uk

Society for Industrial and Organisational Assessment (South Africa) (SIOPSA) – www.siposa.org.za